The Lost Boy

By
Henry van Dyke

The Lost Boy

THAT a child should be lost in Palestine, in the days when Augustus Cæsar was Lord of the World, was no strange thing.

Syria was the most unruly of the Roman provinces, full of adventurers and soldiers of fortune from all nations, troubled by mobs and tumults and rebellions, and infested by landlopers and robbers. Especially in Jerusalem during one of the great Jewish festivals it was most easy for a little stranger to miss his way and

The Lost Boy

be hidden from his friends among the vast throngs of pilgrims and visitors who crowded the city to overflowing and swarmed and streamed through its narrow streets. Amid moving multitudes, ebbing and flowing in restless tides, there were eddies and whirlpools and dark, deep places where a child might be swept away and swallowed up, not only for a few days, but for ever.

But it was strange that this Boy whom my reverie follows now on the dim path of his earliest adventure—it was passing strange that this very Boy should have been lost even for a few hours.

For he was the darling of his parents, the treasure of the household, a lad beloved by all who knew him. His young mother hung on him with

The Lost Boy

passionate, mystical joy and hope. He was the apple of her eye. Deep in her soul she kept the memory of angelic words which had come to her while she carried him under her heart —words which made her believe that her firstborn would be the morning-star of Israel and a light unto the Gentiles. So she cherished the Boy and watched over him with tender, unfailing care, as her most precious possession, her living, breathing, growing jewel.

When he reached the age of twelve, and was old enough to make his first journey to the Temple and take part in the national feast of the Passover, she clad him in the garments of youth and made him ready for the four days' pilgrimage from Nazareth to Jerusalem. It was a camping-trip, a won-

The Lost Boy

der-walk, full of variety, with a spice of danger and a feast of delight.

The Boy was the joy of the journey. His keen interest in all things seen and heard was like a refreshing spring of water to the older pilgrims, who had so often traveled the same road that they had forgotten that it might be new every morning. His unwearying vigor and pure gladness as he leaped down the hillsides, or scrambled among the rocks far above the path, or roamed through the fields filling his hands with flowers, was like a merry song that cheered the long miles of the way. He was glad to be alive, and it made the others glad to look at him.

There were eighty or ninety kinsfolk and neighbors, plain rustic men and women, in the little company that

The Lost Boy

set out from Nazareth. The men carried arms to protect the caravan from robbers or marauders on the way. As they wound slowly down the steep, stony way to the plain of Esdraelon the Boy ran ahead, making short cuts, turning aside to find a partridge's nest among the bushes, leaping from rock to rock like a young gazelle, or poising on the edge of some cliff in sheer delight of his own surefootedness.

His lithe body was outlined against the sky; his deep blue eyes (like those of his mother, who was a maid of Bethlehem) sparkled with the joy of living; his long auburn hair was lifted and tossed by the wind of April. But his mother's look followed him anxiously, and her heart often leaped in her throat.

The Lost Boy

"My Son," she said, as they took their noon-meal in the valley at the foot of dark Mount Gilboa, "you must be more careful. Your feet might slip."

"Mother," answered the Boy, "I am truly very careful. I always put my feet in the places that God has made for them—on the big, strong rocks that will not roll. It is only because I am so glad that you think I am careless."

The tents were pitched, the first night, under the walls of Bethshan, a fortified city of the Romans. Set on a knoll above the river Jordan, the town loomed big and threatening over the little camp of the Galilean pilgrims. But they kept aloof from it, because it was a city of the heathen. Its theaters and temples and palaces

The Lost Boy

were accursed. The tents were indifferent to the city, and when the night opened its star-fields above them and the heavenly lights rose over the mountains of Moab and Samaria the Boy's clear voice joined in the slumber-song of the pilgrims:

"I will lift up mine eyes to the hills,
From whence cometh my help;
My help cometh from the Lord,
Who made heaven and earth.
He will not suffer thy foot to stumble,
He who keepeth thee will not slumber.
Behold, He who guardeth Israel
Will neither slumber nor sleep."

Then they drew their woolen cloaks over their heads and rested on the ground in peace.

For two days their way led through the wide valley of the Jordan, along the level land that stretched from

The Lost Boy

the mountains to the rough gulch where the river was raging in the jungle. They passed through broad fields of ripe barley and ripening wheat, where the quail scuttled and piped among the thick - growing stalks. There were fruit - orchards and olive-groves on the foothills, and clear streams ran murmuring down through glistening oleander thickets. Wild flowers sprang in every untilled corner; tall spikes of hollyhock, scarlet and blue anemones, clusters of mignonette, rock-roses and cyclamens, purple iris in the moist places, and many - colored spathes of gladiolus growing plentifully among the wheat.

The larks sang themselves into the sky in the early morn. Hotter grew the sun and heavier the air in that

The Lost Boy

long trough below the level of the sea. The song of birds melted away. Only the hawks wheeled on motionless wings above silent fields, watching for the young quail or the little rabbits, hidden among the grain.

The pilgrims plodded on in the heat. Companies of soldiers with glittering arms, merchants with laden mules jingling their bells, groups of ragged thieves and bold beggars met and jostled the peaceful travelers on the road. Once a little band of robbers, riding across the valley to the land of Moab, turned from a distance toward the Nazarenes, circled swiftly around them like hawks, whistling and calling shrilly to one another. But there was small booty in that country caravan, and the men who guarded it looked strong and tough; so the robbers

The Lost Boy

whirled away as swiftly as they had come.

The Boy had stood close to his father in this moment of danger, looking on with surprise at the actions of the horsemen.

"What did those riders want?" he asked.

"All we have," answered the man.

"But it is very little," said the Boy. "Nothing but our clothes and some food for our journey. If they were hungry, why did they not ask of us?"

The man laughed. "These are not the kind that ask," he said, "they are the kind that take—what they will and when they can."

"I do not like them," said the Boy. "Their horses were beautiful, but their faces were hateful—like a jackal that I saw in the gulley behind Naz-

The Lost Boy

areth one night. His eyes were burning red as fire. Those men had fires inside of them."

For the rest of that afternoon he walked more quietly and with thoughtful looks, as if he were pondering the case of men who looked like jackals and had flames within them.

At sunset, when the camp was made outside the gates of the new city of Archelaus, on a hillock among the corn-fields, he came to his mother with his hands full of the long lavender and rose and pale-blue spathes of the gladiolus-lilies.

"Look, mother," he cried, "are they not fine—like the clothes of a king?"

"What do you know of kings?" she answered, smiling. "These are

The Lost Boy

only wild lilies of the field. But a great king, like Solomon, has robes of thick silk, and jewels on his neck and his fingers, and a big crown of gold on his head."

"But that must be very heavy," said the Boy, tossing his head lightly. "It must tire him to wear a crown-thing and such thick robes. Besides, I think the lilies are really prettier. They look just as if they were glad to grow in the field."

The third night they camped among the palm-groves and heavy-odored gardens of Jericho, where Herod's splendid palace rose above the trees. The fourth day they climbed the wild, steep, robber-haunted road from the Jordan valley to the highlands of Judea, and so came at sundown to their camp-ground among friends and

The Lost Boy

neighbors on the closely tented slope of the Mount of Olives, over against Jerusalem.

What an evening that was for the Boy! His first sight of the holy city, the city of the great king, the city lifted up and exalted on the sides of the north, beautiful for situation, the joy of the whole earth! He had dreamed of her glory as he listened at his mother's knee to the wonder-tales of David and Solomon and the brave adventures of the fighting Maccabees. He had prayed for the peace of Jerusalem every night as he kneeled by his bed and lifted his young hands toward the holy place. He had tried a thousand times to picture her strength and her splendor, her marvels and mysteries, her multitude of houses and her vast bul-

The Lost Boy

warks, as he strayed among the humble cottages of Nazareth or sat in the low doorway of his own home.

Now his dream had come true. He looked into the face of Jerusalem, just across the deep, narrow valley of the Kidron, where the shadows of the evening were rising among the tombs. The huge battlemented walls, encircling the double mounts of Zion and Moriah—the vast huddle of white houses, covering hill and hollow with their flat roofs and standing so close together that the streets were hidden among them—the towers, the colonnades, the terraces—the dark bulk of the Roman castle—the marble pillars and glittering roof of the Temple in its broad court on the hilltop —it was a city of iron and ivory and

The Lost Boy

gold, rising clear against the soft saffron and rose and violet of the western sky.

The Boy sat with his mother on the hillside while the sunset waned, and the lights began to twinkle in the city, the stars to glow in the deepening blue. He questioned her eagerly—what is that black tower?—why does the big roof shine so bright?—where was King David's house?—where are we going to-morrow?

"To-morrow," she answered, "you will see. But now it is the sleep-time. Let us sing the psalm that we used to sing at night in Nazareth—but very softly, not to disturb the others—for you know this psalm is not one of the songs of the pilgrimage."

The Lost Boy

So the mother and her Child sang together with low voices:

"In peace will I both lay me down and sleep,
For thou, Lord, makest me dwell in safety."

The tune and the words quieted the Boy. It was like a bit of home in a far land.

The next day was full of wonder and excitement. It was the first day of the Feast, and the myriads of pilgrims crowded through the gates and streets of the city, all straining toward the inclosure of the Temple, within whose walls two hundred thousand people could be gathered. On every side the Boy saw new and strange things: soldiers in their armor, and shops full of costly wares;

The Lost Boy

richly dressed Sadducees with their servants following; Jews from far-away countries, and curious visitors from all parts of the world; ragged children of the city, and painted women of the street, and beggars and outcasts of the lower quarters, and rich ladies with their retinues, and priests in their snowy robes.

The family from Nazareth passed slowly through the confusion, and the Boy, bewildered by the changing scene, longed to get to the Temple, where he thought everything must be quiet and holy. But when they came into the immense outer court, with its porticos and alcoves, he found the confusion worse than ever. For there the money-changers and the buyers and sellers of animals for sacrifice were bargaining and haggling;

The Lost Boy

and the thousands of people were jostling and pushing one another; and the followers of the Pharisees and the Sadducees were disputing; and on many faces he saw that strange look which speaks of a fire in the heart, so that it seemed like a meeting-place of robbers.

His father had bought a lamb for the Passover sacrifice, at one of the stalls in the outer court, and was carrying it on his shoulder. He pressed on through the crowd to the Beautiful Gate, the Boy and his mother following until they came to the Court of the Women. Here the mother stayed, for that was the law —a woman must not go further. But the Boy was now "a son of the Commandment," and he followed his father through the Court of Israel to

The Lost Boy

the entrance of the Court of the Priests. There the little lamb was given to a priest, who carried it away to the great stone altar in the middle of the court.

The Boy could not see what happened then, for the place was crowded and busy. But he heard the blowing of trumpets, and the clashing of cymbals, and the chanting of psalms. Black clouds of smoke went up from the hidden altar; the floor around was splashed and streaked with red. After a long while, as it seemed, the priest brought back the dead body of the lamb, prepared for the Passover supper.

"Is this our little lamb?" asked the Boy as his father took it again upon his shoulder.

The father nodded.

The Lost Boy

"It was a very pretty one," said the Boy. "Did it have to die for us?"

The father looked down at him curiously. "Surely," he said, "it had to be offered on the altar, so that we can keep our feast according to the law of Moses to-night."

"But why," persisted the Boy, "must all the lambs be killed in the Temple? Does God like that? How many do you suppose were brought to the altar to-day?"

"Tens of thousands," answered the father.

"It is a great many," said the Boy, sighing. "I wish one was enough."

He was silent and thoughtful as they made their way through the Court of the Women and found the mother and went back to the camp on the hillside. That night the family

The Lost Boy

ate their Paschal feast, with their loins girded as if they were going on a journey, in memory of the long-ago flight of the Israelites from Egypt. There was the roasted lamb, with bitter herbs, and flat cakes of bread made without yeast. A cup of wine was passed around the table four times. The Boy asked his father the meaning of all these things, and the father repeated the story of the saving of the first-born sons of Israel in that far-off night of terror and death when they came out of Egypt. While the supper was going on, hymns were sung, and when it was ended they all chanted together:

"Oh, give thanks to the Lord, for He is good;
For His loving-kindness endureth for ever."

So the Boy lay down under his striped woolen cloak of blue and white

The Lost Boy

and drifted toward sleep, glad that he was a son of Israel, but sorry when he thought of the thousands of little lambs and the altar floor splashed with red. He wondered if some day God would not give them another way to keep that feast.

The next day of the festival was a Sabbath, on which no work could be done. But the daily sacrifice of the Temple, and all the services and songs and benedictions in its courts, continued as usual, and there was a greater crowd than ever within its walls. As the Boy went thither with his parents they came to a place where a little house was beginning to burn, set on fire by an overturned lamp. The poor people stood by wringing their hands and watching the flames.

The Lost Boy

"Why do they not try to save their house?" cried the Boy.

The father shook his head. "They can do nothing," he answered. "They follow the teaching of the Pharisees, who say that it is unlawful to put out a fire on the Sabbath, because it is a labor."

A little later the Boy saw a cripple with a crutch, sitting in the door of a cottage, looking very sad and lonely.

"Why does he not go with the others," asked the Boy, "and hear the music at the Temple? That would make him happier. Can't he walk?"

"Yes," answered the father, "he can walk on other days, but not on the Sabbath, for he would have to carry his crutch, and that would be labor."

The Lost Boy

All the time he was in the Temple, watching the procession of priests and Levites and listening to the music, the Boy was thinking what the Sabbath meant, and whether it really rested people and made them happier.

The third day of the festival was the offering of the first-fruits of the new year's harvest. That was a joyous day. A sheaf of ripe barley was reaped and carried into the Temple and presented before the high altar with incense and music. The priests blessed the people, and the people shouted and sang for gladness.

The Boy's heart bounded in his breast as he joined in the song and thought of the bright summer begun, and the birds building their nests, and the flowers clothing the hills with beautiful colors, and the wide fields

The Lost Boy

of golden grain waving in the wind. He was happy all day as he walked through the busy streets with his parents, buying some things that were needed for the home in Nazareth; and he was happy at night when he lay down under an olive-tree beside the tent, for the air was warm and gentle, and he fell asleep under the tree, dreaming of what he would see and do to-morrow.

Now comes the secret of the way he was lost—a way so simple that the wonder is that no one has ever dreamed of it before.

The three important days of the Passover were ended, and the time had come when those pilgrims who wished to return to their homes might leave Jerusalem without offense, though it was more commendable

The Lost Boy

to remain through the full seven days. The people from Nazareth were anxious to be gone — they had a long road to travel—then harvests were waiting. While the Boy, tired out, was sleeping under the tree, the question of going home was talked out and decided. They would break camp at sunrise, and, joining with others of their countrymen who were tented around them, they would take the road for Galilee.

But the Boy awoke earlier than any one else the next morning. Before the dawn a linnet in the tree overhead called him with cheerful songs. He was rested by his long sleep. His breath came lightly. The spirit of youth was beating in his limbs. His heart was eager for adventure. He longed for the top of a high

The Lost Boy

hill—for the wide, blue sky—for the world at his feet — such a sight as he had often found in his rambles among the heights near Nazareth. Why not? He would return in time for the next visit to the Temple.

Quietly he stepped among the sleeping-tents in the dark. A footpath led through the shadowy olive-grove, up the hillside, into the open. There the light was clearer, and the breeze that runs before the daybreak was dancing through the grass. The Boy turned to the left, following along one of the sheep-trails that crossed the high, sloping pastures. Then he bore to the right, breasting the long ridge, and passed the summit, running lightly to the eastward until he came to a rounded, rocky knoll.

The Lost Boy

There he sat down among the little bushes to wait for sunrise.

Far beyond the wrinkled wilderness of Tekoa, and the Dead Sea, and the mountain-wall of Moab, the rim of the sky was already tinged with silvery gray. The fading of the stars traveled slowly upward, and the rising of the rose of dawn followed it, until all the east was softly glowing and the deep blue of the central heaven was transfused with turquoise light. Dark in the gulfs and chasms of the furrowed land the night lingered. Bright along the eastern peaks and ridges the coming day, still hidden, revealed itself in a fringe of dazzling gold, like the crest of a long mounting wave. Shoots and flashes of radiance sprang upward from the glittering edge.

The Lost Boy

Streamers of rose-foam and gold-spray floated in the sky. Then over the barrier of the hills the sun surged royally—crescent, half-disk, full-orb—and overlooked the world. The luminous tide flooded the gray villages of Bethany and Bethphage, and all the emerald hills around Bethlehem were bathed in light.

The Boy sat entranced, watching the miracle by which God makes His sun to shine upon the good and the evil. How strange it was that God should do that—bestow an equal light upon those who obeyed Him and those who broke His law! Yet it was splendid, it was King-like to give in that way, with both hands. No, it was Father-like—and that was what the Boy had learned from his mother—that God who made and

The Lost Boy

ruled all things was his Father. It was the name she had taught him to use in his prayers. Not in the great prayers he learned from the book—the name there was Adonai, the Lord, the Almighty. But in the little prayers that he said by himself it was "my Father!" It made the Boy feel strangely happy and strong to say that. The whole world seemed to breathe and glow around him with an invisible presence. For such a Father, for the sake of His love and favor, the Boy felt he could do anything.

More than that, his mother had told him of something special that the Father had for him to do in the world. In the evenings during the journey and when they were going home together from the Temple, she

The Lost Boy

had repeated to him some of the words that the angel-voices had spoken to her heart, and some of the sayings of wise men from the East who came to visit him when he was a baby. She could not understand all the mystery of it; she did not see how it was going to be brought to pass. He was a child of poverty and lowliness; not rich, nor learned, nor powerful. But with God all things were possible. The choosing and calling of the eternal Father were more than everything else. It was fixed in her heart that somehow her Boy was sent to do a great work for Israel. He was the son of God set apart to save his people and bring back the glory of Zion. He was to fulfil the promises made in olden time and bring in the wonderful reign of the Messiah in the world—

The Lost Boy

perhaps as a forerunner and messenger of the great King, or perhaps himself—ah, she did not know! But she believed in her Boy with her whole soul; and she was sure that his Father would show him what to do.

These sayings, coming amid the excitements of his first journey, his visit to the Temple, his earliest sight of the splendor and confusion and misery of the great city, had sunken all the more deeply into the Boy's mind. Excitement does not blur the impressions of youth; it sharpens them, makes them more vivid. Half-covered and hardly noticed at the time, they spring up into life when the quiet hour comes.

So the Boy remembered his mother's words while he lay watching the sunrise. It would be great to

The Lost Boy

make them come true. To help everybody to feel what he felt lying there on the hilltop—that big, free feeling of peace and confidence and not being afraid! To make those robbers in the Jordan valley see how they were breaking the rule of the world and burning out their own hearts! To cleanse the Temple from the things that filled it with confusion and pain, and drive away the brawling buyers and sellers who were spoiling his Father's great house! To go among those poor and wretched and sorrowful folks who swarmed in Jerusalem and teach them that God was their Father too, and that they must not sin and quarrel any more! To find a better way than the priests' and the Pharisees' of making people good! To do great things for Israel

The Lost Boy

—like Moses, like Joshua, like David—or like Daniel, perhaps, who prayed and was not afraid of the lions—or like Elijah and Elisha, who went about speaking to the people and healing them—

The soft tread of bare feet among the bushes behind him roused the Boy. He sprang up and saw a man with a stern face and long hair and beard looking at him mysteriously. The man was dressed in white, with a leathern girdle round his waist, into which a towel was thrust. A leathern wallet hung from his neck, and he leaned upon a long staff.

"Peace be with you, Rabbi," said the Boy, reverently bowing at the stranger's feet. But the man looked at him steadily and did not speak.

The Boy was confused by the si-

The Lost Boy

lence. The man's eyes troubled him with their secret look, but he was not afraid.

"Who are you, sir," he asked, "and what is your will with me? Perhaps you are a master of the Pharisees or a scribe? But no—there are no broad blue fringes on your garments. Are you a priest, then?"

The man shook his head, frowning. "I despise the priests," he answered, "and I abhor their bloody and unclean sacrifices. I am Enoch the Essene, a holy one, a perfect keeper of the law. I live with those who have never defiled themselves with the eating of meat, nor with marriage, nor with wine; but we have all things in common, and we are baptized in pure water every day for the purifying of our wretched bodies, and

The Lost Boy

after that we eat the daily feast of love in the kingdom of the Messiah which is at hand. Thou art called into that kingdom, son; come with me, for thou art called."

The Boy listened with astonishment. Some of the things that the man said—for instance, about the sacrifices and about the nearness of the kingdom—were already in his heart. But other things puzzled and bewildered him.

"My mother says that I am called," he answered, "but it is to serve Israel and to help the people. Where do you live, sir, and what is it that you do for the people?"

"We live among the hills of that wilderness," he answered, pointing to the south, "in the oasis of Engedi. There are palm-trees and springs of

The Lost Boy

water, and we keep ourselves pure, bathing before we eat and offering our food of bread and dates as a sacrifice to God. We all work together, and none of us has anything that he calls his own. We do not go up to the Temple nor enter the synagogues. We have forsaken the uncleanness of the world and all the impure ways of men. Our only care is to keep ourselves from defilement. If we touch anything that is forbidden we wash our hands and wipe them with this towel that hangs from our girdle. We alone are serving the kingdom. Come, live with us, for I think thou art chosen."

The Boy thought for a while before he answered. "Some of it is good, my master," he said, "but the rest of it is far away from my thoughts.

The Lost Boy

Is there nothing for a man to do in the world but to think of himself—either in feasting and uncleanness as the heathen do, or in fasting and purifying yourself as you do? How can you serve the kingdom if you turn away from the people? They do not see you or hear you. You are separate from them—just as if you were dead without dying. You can do nothing for them. No, I do not want to come with you and live at Engedi. I think my Father will show me something better to do."

"Your Father!" said Enoch the Essene. "Who is He?"

"Surely," answered the Boy, "He is the same as yours. He that made us and made all that we see—the great world for us to live in."

"Dust," said the man, with a dark-

The Lost Boy

er frown—"dust and ashes! It will all perish, and thou with it. Thou art not chosen—not pure!"

With that he went away down the hill; and the Boy, surprised and grieved at his rude parting, wondered a little over the meaning of his words, and then went back as quickly as he could toward the tents.

When he came to the olive-grove they were gone! The sun was already high, and his people had departed hours ago. In the hurry and bustle of breaking camp each of the parents had supposed that the Boy was with the other, or with some of the friends and neighbors, or perhaps running along the hillside above them as he used to do. So they went their way cheerfully, not knowing that they had left their son behind.

The Lost Boy

When the Boy saw what had happened he was surprised and troubled, but not frightened. He did not know what to do. He might hasten after them, but he could not tell which way to go. He was not even sure that they had gone home; for they had talked of paying a visit to their relatives in the south before returning to Nazareth; and some of the remaining pilgrims to whom he turned for news of his people said that they had taken the southern road from the Mount of Olives, going toward Bethlehem.

The Boy was at a loss, but he was not disheartened, nor even cast down. He felt that somehow all would be well with him; he would be taken care of. They would come back for him in good time. Meanwhile there

The Lost Boy

were kind people here who would give him food and shelter. There were boys in the other camps with whom he could play. Best of all, he could go again to the city and the Temple. He could see more of the wonderful things there, and watch the way the people lived, and find out why so many of them seemed sad or angry, and a few proud and scornful, and almost all looked unsatisfied. Perhaps he could listen to some of the famous rabbis who taught the people in the courts of the Temple and learn from them about the things which his Father had chosen him to do.

So he went down the hill and toward the Sheep Gate by which he had always gone into the city. Outside the gate a few boys about his own

The Lost Boy

age, with a group of younger children, were playing games.

"Look there," they cried — "a stranger! Let us have some fun with him. Halloo, Country, where do you come from?"

"From Galilee," answered the Boy.

"Galilee is where all the fools live," cried the children. "Where is your home? What is your name?"

He told them pleasantly, but they laughed at his country way of speaking and mimicked his pronunciation.

"Yalilean! Yalilean!" they cried. "You can't talk. Can you play? Come and play with us."

So they played together. First, they had a mimic wedding-procession. Then they made believe that the bridegroom was killed by a robber, and they had a mock funeral.

The Lost Boy

The Boy took always the lowest part. He was the hired mourner who followed the body, wailing; he was the flute-player who made music for the wedding-guests to dance to.

So readily did he enter into the play that the children at first were pleased with him. But they were not long contented with anything. Some of them would dance no more for the wedding; others would lament no more for the funeral. Their caprices made them quarrelsome.

"Yalilean fool," they cried, "you play it all wrong. You spoil the game. We are tired of it. Can you run? Can you throw stones?"

So they ran races; and the Boy, trained among the hills, outran the others. But they said he did not keep to the course. Then they threw

The Lost Boy

stones; and the Boy threw farther and straighter than any of the rest. This made them angry.

Whispering together, they suddenly hurled a shower of stones at him. One struck his shoulder, another made a long cut on his cheek. Wiping away the blood with his sleeve, he turned silently and ran to the Sheep Gate, the other boys chasing him with loud shouts.

He darted lightly through the crowd of animals and people that thronged the gateway, turning and dodging with a sure foot among them and running up the narrow street that led to the sheep-market. The cries of his pursuers grew fainter behind him. Among the stalls of the market he wound this way and that way like a hare before the hounds.

The Lost Boy

At last he had left them out of sight and hearing.

Then he ceased running and wandered blindly on through the northern quarter of the city. The sloping streets were lined with bazaars and noisy workshops. The Roman soldiers from the castle were sauntering to and fro. Women in rich attire, with ear-rings and gold chains, passed by with their slaves. Open market-places were still busy, though the afternoon trade was slackening.

But the Boy was too tired and faint with hunger and heavy at heart to take an interest in these things. He turned back toward the gate, and, missing his way a little, came to a great pool of water, walled in with white stone, with five porticos around it. In some of these porticos there

The Lost Boy

were a few people lying upon mats. But one of the porches was empty, and here the Boy sat down.

He was worn out. His cheek was bleeding again, and the drops trickled down his neck. He went down the broad steps to the pool to wash away the blood. But he could not do it very well. His head ached too much. So he crept back to the porch, unwound his little turban, curled himself in a corner on the hard stones, his head upon his arm, and went sound asleep.

He was awakened by a voice calling him, a hand laid upon his shoulder. He looked up and saw the face of a young woman, dark-eyed, red-lipped, only a few years older than himself. She was clad in silk, with a veil of gauze over her head, gold coins in her

The Lost Boy

hair, and a vial of alabaster hanging by a gold chain around her neck. A sweet perfume like the breath of roses came from it as she moved. Her voice was soft and kind.

"Poor boy," she said, "you are wounded; some one has hurt you. What are you doing here. You look like a little brother that I had long ago. Come with me. I will take care of you."

The Boy rose and tried to go with her. But he was stiff and sore; he could hardly walk; his head was swimming. The young woman beckoned to a Nubian slave who followed her. He took the Boy in his big black arms and so carried him to a pleasant house with a garden.

There were couches and cushions there, in a marble court around a

The Lost Boy

fountain. There were servants who brought towels and ointments. The young woman bathed the Boy's wound and his feet. The servants came with food, and she made him eat of the best. His eyes grew bright again, and the color came into his cheeks. He talked to her of his life in Nazareth, of the adventures of his first journey, and of the way he came to be lost.

She listened to him intently, as if there were some strange charm in his simple talk. Her eyes rested upon him with pleasure. A new look swept over her face. She leaned close to him.

"Stay with me, boy," she murmured, "for I want you. Your people are gone. You shall sleep here tonight—you shall live with me and I

The Lost Boy

will be good to you—I will teach you to love me."

The Boy moved back a little and looked at her with wide eyes, as if she were saying something that he could not understand.

"But you have already been good to me, sister," he answered, "and I love you already, even as your brother did. Is your husband here? Will he come soon, so that we can all say the prayer of thanksgiving together for the food?"

Her look changed again; her eyes filled with pain and sorrow; she shrank back and turned away her face.

"I have no husband," she said. "Ah, boy, innocent boy, you do not understand. I eat the bread of shame and live in the house of wickedness.

The Lost Boy

I am a sinner, a sinner of the city. How could I pray?"

With that she fell a-sobbing, rocking herself to and fro, and the tears ran through her fingers like rain. The Boy looked at her, astonished and pitiful. He moved nearer to her, after a moment, and spoke softly.

"I am very sorry, sister," he said; and as he spoke he felt her tears falling on his feet. "I am more sorry than I ever was in my life. It must be dreadful to be a sinner. But sinners can pray, for God is our Father, and fathers know how to forgive. I will stay with you and teach you some of the things my mother has taught me."

She looked up and caught his hand and kissed it. She wiped away her tears, and rose, pushing back her hair.

The Lost Boy

"No, dear little master," she said, "you shall not stay in this house— not an hour. It is not fit for you. My Nubian shall lead you back to the gate, and you will return to your friends outside of the city, and you will forget one whom you comforted for a moment."

The Boy turned back as he stood in the doorway. "No," he said. "I will not forget you. I will always remember your love and kindness. Will you learn to pray, and give up being a sinner?"

"I will try," she answered; "you have made me want to try. Go in peace. God knows what will become of me."

"God knows, sister," replied the Boy, gravely. "Abide in peace."

So he went out into the dusk with

The Lost Boy

the Nubian and found the camp on the hillside and a shelter in one of the friendly tents, where he slept soundly and woke refreshed in the morning.

This day he would not spend in playing and wandering. He would go straight to the Temple, to find some of the learned teachers who gave instruction there, and learn from them the wisdom that he needed in order to do his work for his Father.

As he went he thought about the things that had befallen him yesterday. Why had the man dressed in white despised him? Why had the city children mocked him and chased him away with stones? Why was the strange woman who had been so kind to him afterward so unhappy and so hopeless?

There must be something in the

The Lost Boy

world that he did not understand, something evil and hateful and miserable that he had never felt in himself. But he felt it in the others, and it made him so sorry, so distressed for them, that it seemed like a heavy weight, a burden on his own heart. It was like the work of those demons, of whom his mother had told him, who entered into people and lived inside of them, like worms eating away a fruit. Only these people of whom he was thinking did not seem to have a demon that took hold of them and drove them mad and made them foam at the mouth and cut themselves with stones, like a man he once saw in Galilee. This was something larger and more mysterious—like the hot wind that sometimes blew from the south and made

The Lost Boy

people gloomy and angry—like the rank weeds that grew in certain fields, and if the sheep fed there they dropped and died.

The Boy felt that he hated this unknown, wicked, unhappy thing more than anything else in the world. He would like to save people from it. He wanted to fight against it, to drive it away. It seemed as if there were a spirit in his heart saying to him, "This is what you must do, you must fight against this evil, you must drive out the darkness, you must be a light, you must save the people—this is your Father's work for you to do."

But how? He did not know. That was what he wanted to find out. And he went into the Temple hoping that the teachers there would tell him.

The Lost Boy

He found the vast Court of the Gentiles, as it had been on his first visit, swarming with people. Jews and Syrians and foreigners of many nations were streaming into it through the eight open gates, meeting and mingling and eddying round in confused currents, bargaining and haggling with the merchants and money-changers, crowding together around some group where argument had risen to a violent dispute, drifting away again in search of some new excitement.

The morning sacrifice was ended, but the sound of music floated out from the inclosed courts in front of the altar, where the more devout worshipers were gathered. The Roman soldiers of the guard paced up and down, or leaned tranquilly upon

The Lost Boy

their spears, looking with indifference or amused contempt upon the turbulent scenes of the holy place where they were set to keep the peace and prevent the worshipers from attacking one another.

The Boy turned into the long, cool cloisters, with their lofty marble columns and carved roofs of wood, which ran around the inside of the walls. Here he found many groups of people, walking in the broad aisles between the pillars, or seated in the alcoves of Solomon's Porch around the teachers who were instructing them. From one to another of these open schools he wandered, listening eagerly to the different rabbis and doctors of the law.

Here one was reading from the Torah and explaining the laws about

The Lost Boy

the food which a Jew must not eat, and the things which he must not do on the Sabbath. Here another was expounding the doctrine of the Pharisees about the purifying of the sacred vessels in the Temple; while another, a Sadducee, was disputing with him scornfully and claiming that the purification of the priests was the only important thing. "You would wash that which needs no washing," he cried, "the Golden Candlestick, one day in every week! Next you will want to wash the sun for fear an unclean ray of light may fall on the altar!"

Other teachers were reciting from the six books of the Talmud which the Pharisees were making to expound the law. Others repeated the histories of Israel, recounted the brave

The Lost Boy

deeds of the Maccabees, or read from the prophecies of Enoch and Daniel. Others still were engaged in political debate: the Zealots talking fiercely of the misdeeds of the house of Herod and the outrages committed by the Romans; the Sadducees contemptuously mocking at the hopes of the revolutionists and showing that the dream of freedom for Judea was foolish. "Freedom," they said, "belongs to those who are well protected. We have the Temple and priesthood because Rome takes care of us." To this the Zealots answered, angrily, "Yes, the priesthood belongs to you unbelieving Sadducees; that is why you are content with it. Look, now, at the place where you let Herod hang an accursed eagle of gold on the front of Jehovah's House."

The Lost Boy

So from group to group the Boy passed, listening intently, but hearing little to his purpose. All day long he listened, now to one, now to another, completely absorbed by what he heard, yet not satisfied. Late in the afternoon he came into the quietest part of Solomon's Porch, where two large companies were seated around their respective teachers, separated from each other by a distance of four or five columns.

As he stood on the edge of the first company, whose rabbi was a lean, dark-bearded, stern little man, the Boy was spoken to by a stranger at his side, who asked him what he sought in the Temple.

"Wisdom," answered the Boy. "I am looking for some one to give a light to my path."

The Lost Boy

"That is what I am seeking, too," said the stranger, smiling. "I am a Greek, and I desire wisdom. Let us see if we can get it from this teacher. Listen."

He made his way to the center of the circle and stood before the stern little man.

"Master," said the Greek, "I am willing to become thy disciple if thou wilt teach me the whole law while I stand before thee thus—on one foot."

The rabbi looked at him angrily, and, lifting up his stick, smote him sharply across the leg. "That is the whole law for mockers," he cried. The stranger limped away amid the laughter of the crowd.

"But the little man was too angry; he did not see that I was in earnest," said he, as he came back to the Boy.

The Lost Boy

"Now let us go to the next school and see if the master is any better."

So they went to the second company, which was seated around a very old man, with long, snowy beard and a gentle face. The stranger took his place as before, standing on one foot, and made the same request. The rabbi's eyes twinkled and his lips were smiling as he answered promptly:

"Do nothing to thy neighbor that thou wouldst not he should do to thee, this is the whole law; all the rest follows from this."

"Well," said the stranger, returning, "what think you of this teacher and his wisdom? Is it better?"

"It is far better," replied the Boy, eagerly; "it is the best of all I have

The Lost Boy

heard to-day. I am coming back to hear him to-morrow. Do you know his name?"

"I think it is Hillel," answered the Greek, "and he is a learned man, the master of the Sanhedrim. You will do well, young Jew, to listen to such a man. Socrates could not have answered me better. But now the sun is near setting. We must go our ways. Farewell."

In the tent of his friends the Boy found welcome and a supper, but no news of his parents. He told his experiences in the Temple, and the friends heard him, wondering at his discernment. They were in doubt whether to let him go again the next day; but he begged so earnestly, arguing that they could tell his parents where he was if they should come to

The Lost Boy

the camp seeking him, that finally he won consent.

He was in Solomon's Porch long before the schools had begun to assemble. He paced up and down under the triple colonnade thinking what questions he should ask the master.

The company that gathered around Hillel that day was smaller, but there were more scribes and doctors of the law among them, and they were speaking of the kingdom of the Messiah—the thing that lay nearest to the Boy's heart. He took his place in the midst of them, and they made room for him, for they liked young disciples and encouraged them to ask after knowledge.

It was the prophecy of Daniel that they were discussing, and the ques-

The Lost Boy

tion was whether these things were written of the First Messiah or of the Second Messiah; for many of the doctors held that there must be two, and that the first would die in battle, but the second would put down all his enemies and rule over the world.

'Rabbi," asked the Boy, "if the first was really the Messiah, could not God raise him up again and send him back to rule?"

"You ask wisely, son," answered Hillel, "and I think the prophets tell us that we must hope for only one Messiah. This book of Daniel is full of heavenly words, but it is not counted among the prophets whose writings are gathered in the Scripture. Which of them have you read, and which do you love most, my son?"

"Isaiah," said the Boy, "because

The Lost Boy

he says God will have mercy with everlasting-kindness. But I love Daniel, too, because he says they that turn many to righteousness shall shine as the stars for ever and ever. But I do not understand what he says about the times and a half-time and the days and the seasons before the coming of Messiah."

With this there rose a dispute among the doctors about the meaning of those sayings, and some explained them one way and some another, but Hillel sat silent. At last he said:

"It is better to hope and to wait patiently for Him than to reckon the day of His coming. For if the reckoning is wrong, and He does not come, then men despair, and no longer make ready for Him."

The Lost Boy

"How does a man make ready for Him, Rabbi?" asked the Boy.

"By prayer, son, and by study of the law, and by good works, and by sacrifices."

"But when He comes He will rule over the whole world, and how can all the world come to the Temple to sacrifice?"

"A way will be provided," answered the old man, "though I do not know how it will be. And there are offerings of the heart as well as of the altar. It is written, 'I will have mercy and not sacrifice.'"

"Will His kingdom be for the poor as well as for the rich, and for the ignorant as well as for the wise?"

"Yes, it will be more for the poor than for the rich. But it will not be for the ignorant, my son. For he

The Lost Boy

who does not know the law cannot be pious."

"But, Rabbi," said the Boy, eagerly, "will He not have mercy on them just because they are ignorant? Will He not pity them as a shepherd pities his sheep when they are silly and go astray?"

"He is not only a Shepherd," answered Hillel, firmly, "but a great King. They must all keep the law, even as it is written and as the elders have taught it to us. There is no other way."

The Boy was silent for a time, while the others talked of the law, and of the Torah, and of the Talmud in which Hillel in these days was writing down the traditions of the elders. When there was an opportunity he spoke again.

The Lost Boy

"Rabbi, if most of the people should be poor and ignorant when the Messiah came, so ignorant that they did not even know Him, wouldn't He save them just because they were poor?"

Hillel looked at the Boy with love, and hesitated before he answered.

At that moment a man and a woman came through the colonnade with hurried steps. The man stopped at the edge of the circle, astonished at what he saw. But the woman came into the center and put her arm around the Boy.

"My boy," she cried, "why hast thou done this to us? See how sorrowful thou hast made me and thy father, looking everywhere for thee."

"Mother," he answered, "why did you look everywhere for me with sor-

The Lost Boy

row? Did you not know that I would be in my Father's house? Must I not begin to think of the things my Father wants me to do?"

Thus the lost Boy was found again, and went home with his parents to Nazareth. The old rabbi blessed him as he left the Temple.

But had he really been lost, or was he finding his way?

THE END

Made in United States
Orlando, FL
10 November 2023